A MARKED MAN
THE ASSASSINATION OF MALCOLM X

MATT DOEDEN

TFCB

TWENTY-FIRST CENTURY BOOKS / MINNEAPOLIS

Twenty-First Century Books
A division of Lerner Publishing Group, Inc.
241 First Avenue North
Minneapolis, MN 55401 U.S.A.

Website address: www.lernerbooks.com

Library of Congress Cataloging-in-Publication Data

Doeden, Matt.
A marked man: the assassination of Malcolm X /
by Matt Doeden.
p.   cm.
Includes bibliographical references and index.
ISBN 978-0-7613-5484-0 (lib. bdg. : alk. paper)
1. X, Malcolm, 1925-1965—Juvenile literature. 2. Black
Muslims—Biography—Juvenile literature. 3. African
Americans—Biography. I. Title.
BP223.Z8L5733357 2013
320.54'6092—dc23 [B]   2012018074

Manufactured in the United States of America
1 – PP – 12/31/12

INTRODUCTION

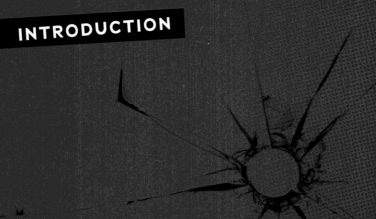

The gentleman you know as Malcolm X is dead.

COLUMBIA UNIVERSITY MEDICAL CENTER REPRESENTATIVE,
FEBRUARY 21, 1965

When the world learned on February 21, 1965, that thirty-nine-year-old civil rights activist Malcolm X had been assassinated, few Americans were truly surprised. Some were appalled by the violence of the murder—he had been shot in public in New York by three men at point-blank range. Others were deeply saddened at the news of the death of an inspiring voice for social justice. Still others—blacks and whites alike—may have even felt a sense of relief at the passing of the controversial figure.

But no one who had followed the life and career of Malcolm X was truly shocked by the news. For many, the question surrounding the African American civil rights leader wasn't whether he would be killed but when.

Malcolm's assassination on February 21, 1965, captured headlines across the country the following morning. The *New York Daily News (left)* splashed the story across the entire front page.

No one had understood the danger better than Malcolm X himself. Ever since his 1964 split with the Nation of Islam (NOI)—a radical religious movement preaching justice for African Americans—Malcolm had referred to himself as a marked man. He knew that his enemies within the NOI would use violence to silence him. "I live like a man who's already dead," he had said in an interview shortly before his death.

Even knowing the danger, Malcolm X did not hesitate to spread his message of black power and social change. On the afternoon of his

New York City to speak about his efforts to unite blacks across the United States and Africa. He had known that every public appearance could be his last. Even his home, which had been firebombed the week before, wasn't safe.

As he spoke, commotion in the audience interrupted him. As Malcolm tried to calm the crowd, three men opened fire. Shots from a shotgun and two automatic pistols rang out, knocking Malcolm to the floor behind his lectern. Malcolm was rushed to a nearby hospital. His injuries were so massive that doctors could do nothing to save him. He was pronounced dead fifteen minutes later.

In the panic and confusion that followed the assassination, all but one of the armed men escaped. This man, Talmadge Hayer, was shot in the leg by Malcolm's security team and was later picked up by the police. News of Malcolm's death spread quickly and drew a wide range of responses from outrage to relief. Yet one question haunted the nation. Who were Malcolm X's killers? Half a century later, the answer remains elusive.

Malcolm posed for this portrait on February 16, 1965, the week before his assassination.

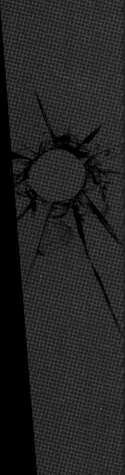

CHAPTER 1
THE MAKING OF A LEADER

I'm not interested in being American, because America has never been interested in me.

MALCOLM X, 1962

The Little family welcomed a baby boy, Malcolm, on May 19, 1925, in Omaha, Nebraska. He came into a world of racial tension and violence. About a month before his birth, his mother, Louise, was visited by members of the Ku Klux Klan (KKK). The KKK was an organization of white supremacists who often used violence against blacks and other minorities. The Klan members had come because Malcolm's father, the Reverend Earl Little, was

The Ku Klux Klan terrorized the Little family and other African American citizens. Klan members attended Klan functions in white robes and hats for anonymity.

outspoken in his support of the rights of black Americans. He had joined a controversial group called the Universal Negro Improvement Association (UNIA), which called for black Americans to return to Africa to form a new nation. Members of the Klan despised this message and came to the house with the intention of lynching (hanging) him.

But Earl Little was not home that night. Louise Little was there with their three children. She was visibly pregnant (with Malcolm). The Klansmen did not hurt Louise or the children, but they broke windows in the home and left Louise with a warning. The Little family wasn't welcome in Omaha, the men said. If the Littles valued their lives, they would leave.

The Littles did just that soon after Malcolm was born. The family moved to Milwaukee, Wisconsin, with Malcolm and three older siblings. In time three other siblings were born. Malcolm also had three half siblings from Earl's previous marriage. These siblings lived in Boston, Massachusetts.

HARD LESSONS

The Little family didn't stay in Milwaukee long. Shortly after Malcolm's fourth birthday, the family moved to Lansing, Michigan. Earl and Louise bought a farmhouse on the outskirts of the city. Whites opposed to having a black family live in the area filed a lawsuit to reverse the sale. They argued that the deed for the land allowed only Caucasian (white) people to live there. Earl wasn't willing to give up, however. He was going to fight for his family's right to live in the house.

Two weeks later, Malcolm was awakened in the middle of the night. Two white men had set the family's house on fire. Earl shot at the men as they fled. Malcolm later recalled standing outside, crying and yelling as he and his family watched their house burn to the ground.

The family then moved to East Lansing, where they again faced racial harassment. They finally settled outside of town. Earl and Louise fought often, and Earl sometimes beat his wife. In his autobiography, Malcolm recalled that Earl was often brutal with his children as well. Malcolm alone was spared. Later in life, Malcolm wondered why he had been favored. He concluded that because he had the lightest skin among his siblings, his father treated him less severely. At this time in U.S. history, many people judged African Americans by the darkness of their skin color. The lighter the skin, the less discrimination a person faced.

Another sign of Earl's favoritism was that Malcolm was the only child Earl took with him to UNIA meetings. Young Malcolm couldn't have understood the issues under discussion at these meetings. All the same, he was exposed to civil rights issues from a very young age.

A follower of Marcus Garvey, founder of the Universal Negro Improvement Association, stands outside of the UNIA club in New York in the 1940s.

Poverty was a way of life for the Littles and for the other African Americans of the Lansing area. It was the beginning of the Great Depression (1929–1942). The United States and the rest of the world were suffering through severe economic difficulties. Jobs were hard to come by, particularly for African Americans. Earl made a little money from preaching and from odd jobs, and the family raised its own food, including vegetables and chickens.

At the age of five, Malcolm began to attend school. The Little children were the only African American students in the school. The other children called them racially insulting names, but Malcolm and his siblings were so used to hearing these terms that they didn't think of them as slurs.

SCREAMS IN THE NIGHT

In September 1931, six-year-old Malcolm was once again awakened in the middle of the night. His mother was screaming, and the police were in the house.

Earl had been run over by a streetcar. His body, cut almost in half, had been found near a track that ran between Lansing and East Lansing. Some said it was an accident. But Louise was sure that Earl had been killed by a local white supremacist group called the Black Legion. Members of the legion did not like Earl's message of African American unity and pride. They felt whites were superior to blacks.

Members of the Black Legion in Detroit await trial for the murder of a local man in the 1930s. The Black Legion got its start in Ohio in the 1920s as a security force for the KKK.

Without Earl, the Little family was left with no dependable source of income. So Louise took housekeeping jobs in white households. Because of her light complexion (Louise's father was white), many people assumed that Louise was white. When they found out that she was black, she was often fired. Many whites didn't want a black woman in their homes. Malcolm's older brother Wilfred quit school so he could look for work and earn money for the family. Even that was not enough, and the family went on welfare—a humiliating experience for Louise.

Meanwhile, young Malcolm was showing emotional scars from the death of his father. He developed a terrible fear of the dark and was tormented by fears of sudden death in the night. In addition, he became a troublemaker. He and his brother Philbert picked fights at school. Malcolm took to stealing from local stores. And although he had always been a good student, he began clashing with his teachers.

TEEN YEARS

The stress of losing Earl and having to raise seven children by herself became too much for Louise. When Malcolm was about thirteen, she suffered a mental breakdown and was officially declared insane. Malcolm and his siblings were placed in foster homes. Malcolm adapted to the change as well as could be expected. He was doing reasonably well in school, both socially and academically. Still, he had a lot of energy and no outlet for it. So he began to act out in school. In one of his classes, he put a thumbtack on the teacher's chair, leading to an expulsion that again changed his life.

Malcolm was placed in a detention home in Mason, about 12 miles (19 kilometers) from Lansing. It was run by Mr. and Mrs. Swerlin, a white couple. Malcolm found the couple to be kind and well-meaning yet unknowingly insensitive. They often used insulting racial language in the home. Despite the racist language, the couple liked Malcolm and he liked them. Only later did he come to the conclusion that the Swerlin family thought of him as a mascot, more like a pet than a child. It was an eye-opening realization for Malcolm. It taught him that racism wasn't always paired with hatred and violence. Racism could also come in the form of kindness and ignorance.

In time, Malcolm was enrolled at Mason Junior High. Mason was a mainly white city, and Malcolm was the only African American in his class. Malcolm was very popular and was voted class president. He excelled in his classes and played on the school's basketball team. Mrs. Swerlin also got Malcolm a job washing dishes.

Malcolm felt as if he were on top of the world. He later reflected that during those years, he had been trying his hardest to ignore his heritage and to become a white person. There were always reminders of who he was, however. Some of his teachers told racially insulting jokes in class. At school dances, Malcolm knew better than to dance with a white girl. At the time, strict social taboos forbade African American men from having any kind of contact with white women. Since there were no black girls his age, Malcolm had no one to dance with. He would instead stand off to the side and find an excuse to leave early.

RACIAL PRIDE

Around the end of Malcolm's seventh-grade year, his half sister Ella visited the Littles. She made an immediate impact on Malcolm. Ella carried herself differently from any African American woman Malcolm had known. She was proud of herself and of her race. She did not try to act as if she were white, and she showed no shame in her dark complexion. He later commented that he had never before been that impressed by anyone. Ella invited Malcolm to visit her in Boston for the summer of 1940, and he accepted.

Ella was at the center of black society in Boston. She introduced Malcolm to many successful African Americans. It opened his eyes to the larger world and forever changed the way he thought about his home in Michigan. Even when he returned to Mason, he found himself wishing to be back in Boston around the educated, successful black people he had met there.

Malcolm worked hard at his studies. One of his favorite teachers encouraged students to make something of their lives. One day, the teacher asked Malcolm what he wanted to be. Malcolm said he'd like to be a lawyer. The teacher scoffed at the suggestion. He told Malcolm to be realistic and that carpentry was a better goal for him.

Those words were like a slap in the face. Malcolm had worked so hard to fit in and to earn good marks in class. Suddenly, he realized that none of it mattered. Even if he was one of the smartest students in class, many people would never see him as an equal.

Just like that, Malcolm's goal of fitting into white society came crashing down around him. It seemed hopeless, and he was no longer willing to fight for it.

HITTING THE STREETS

Malcolm's attitude had changed. He was unhappy and distrustful of whites. Soon after, he moved to Boston to live with Ella.

Malcolm spent time in both rich and poor Boston neighborhoods. He felt more comfortable in the poorer neighborhoods. There he noticed young African American men dressed in wild zoot suits with their hair

This movie still from *Malcolm X* (1992) shows Denzel Washington as Malcolm wearing a zoot suit during his early days in Boston. Malcolm moved to Boston in 1940 to live with his sister Ella.

straightened and greased in a style called the conk. Their flashy style was a way of embracing their place—or lack of place—in white society. Young Malcolm was impressed. He soon adopted the style as his own.

He met one young man who went by the nickname Shorty. Like Malcolm, Shorty was from Lansing. Shorty took Malcolm under his wing and helped him get a job shining shoes in the Roseland State Ballroom. Over the next few years, Malcolm bounced from job to job. He was a drugstore clerk and a busboy in a restaurant. At the age of sixteen, Ella helped him get a job with the railroad as a kitchen helper. Railroad jobs paid well. One of the routes he worked on was a train from Boston to New York. When Malcolm first visited Harlem, a black neighborhood in New York, his perspective changed again. Harlem was alive with African Americans of all social standing. This was where Malcolm wanted to be.

HARLEM

Malcolm loved Harlem. He went out to nightclubs and bars, including one called Small's Paradise. The year was 1942, and the United States had recently entered World War II (1939–1945). The war had helped to revitalize the nation's economy, and with so many young men heading off to war, jobs were suddenly plentiful.

Malcolm soon moved to Harlem and got a job as a waiter at Small's Paradise. He loved spending time there and was, at first, a model employee. Malcolm made good money on tips but gambled much of it away playing numbers (an illegal lottery-like game). He was later fired after he offered to find a prostitute for an undercover law enforcement officer.

Malcolm turned to crime. Detroit Red, as Malcolm was nicknamed (for his home state and the red tint to his hair), sold marijuana on the streets and smoked plenty of it himself. He ran numbers, selling entries into the illegal lottery game. He even turned to robbery. Yet even as a petty criminal, he never stopped studying people. And through it all, his distrust of and disdain for white people—especially white men—grew.

Small's Paradise was an integrated club in Harlem that was open from the 1920s to the 1980s. It featured live jazz music and a dance floor.

In time, Malcolm got into a dispute over money with another street hustler. It was time to leave Harlem and let things cool down for a bit. If one of his rivals didn't get to him first, it was only a matter of time before the police did.

"Everything was building up, closing in on me," Malcolm said in his autobiography. "For four years, up to that point, I'd been lucky enough, or slick enough, to escape jail, or even getting arrested. . . . But I knew that any minute now something had to give."

LOCKED UP

Malcolm returned to Boston, where he and some friends turned to burglarizing homes. He was eventually caught trying to sell a stolen watch. At the age of twenty, Malcolm was sentenced to eight to ten years in prison.

In February 1946, Malcolm began serving his sentence at Charlestown State Prison as Prisoner No. 22843. The prison stank. Malcolm and other

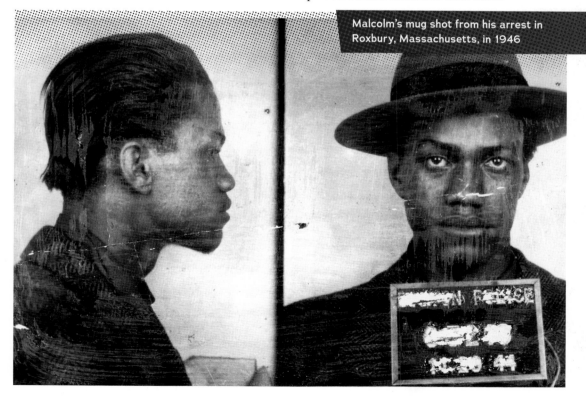

Malcolm's mug shot from his arrest in Roxbury, Massachusetts, in 1946

prisoners had to use buckets as toilets, which they emptied each day. Prisoners had little to keep them busy. This gave Malcolm a lot of time to think.

He spent time in his tiny cell cursing at God and the Bible. He was so angry at the God of Christianity, which he came to view as a white person's religion, that his fellow inmates took to calling him Satan.

In time, Malcolm met a prisoner named Bimbi. Bimbi was thoughtful and articulate. He talked to Malcolm about atheism (the belief that God does not exist) and helped Malcolm tame his own rage. Bimbi also convinced Malcolm to take classes offered to inmates. Malcolm started by studying English. He moved on to a wide range of subjects, from Latin to history to literature. He continued his studies after he was transferred to Concord Prison and then later to the Norfolk Prison Colony.

JOINING THE NATION

Meanwhile, Malcolm's brothers Reginald and Philbert had converted to the religion of Islam. They told Malcolm about an Islamic group in the United States called the Nation of Islam. The group wasn't just about religion. It was also a political movement among black people to fight for economic, political, and social justice for African Americans. The religion appealed to Malcolm. In time, he devoted himself to Allah (the Arabic word for God). And he wanted to be a Black Muslim, as the members of NOI called themselves. So he wrote a letter from prison to the head of the Nation of Islam, Elijah Muhammad. Muhammad responded, asking Malcolm to join the movement.

From that moment, Malcolm felt that he had a place in the world. He no longer wanted to be a petty criminal. He wanted to be a better man,

"All praise is due to Allah that I went to Boston when I did. If I hadn't, I'd probably still be a brainwashed black Christian."

MALCOLM X, CA. 1963

THE NATION OF ISLAM

The Nation of Islam was founded by Wallace Fard Muhammad in Michigan in 1930. The group was based loosely on the principles of the religion of Islam and members believed that Wallace Muhammad was an incarnation of Allah. Elijah Muhammad was one of Wallace Muhammad's most loyal followers. He took control of the organization after Wallace Muhammad's disappearance in 1934.

The Nation of Islam believes that black people were the original humans. In their worldview, a group of twenty-four black scientists was in charge of the world. A rogue scientist called Yakub used a selective breeding program to create the world's other races. The culmination of his project was the white man, an evil race of devils. The white man, according to a prophecy, would come into power for six thousand years before the black man would regain status as the most powerful race. In the twenty-first century, most members of the NOI work toward fulfilling this prophecy.

Mainstream Muslims, however, reject the Nation of Islam as a true Islamic organization largely because it is mostly a social and political organization rather than a religious one. Its purpose has always been to gain rights and promote education for blacks in the United States. These were the goals that drew many of its members, including Malcolm.

The modern NOI stands for a few main principles, including freedom and equality for all black Muslims. The group also advocates for a new nation for the descendants of former slaves in America, with land provided by the descendants of former slave owners. The group does not support interracial marriage.

and he wanted to make a difference in the world. Much of his passion was fueled by a growing hatred of whites, and he was determined to channel that hatred into a revolution. The NOI offered him a way to do all of this.

The Nation of Islam believed that the first step in fighting for racial justice was education. The more its members knew and understood about the world and its history, the better they would be able to defend and promote their cause. So Malcolm joined a prison debating society to practice articulating and defending his views. He read constantly. He even read—and copied by hand—a dictionary, marveling at all the new words he was learning. He wrote to Muhammad almost daily. He eagerly talked to his fellow inmates about the Nation of Islam and its mission.

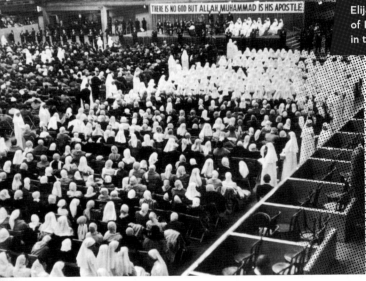

Elijah Muhammad speaks at a Nation of Islam gathering in Chicago, Illinois, in the 1960s.

In August 1952, twenty-seven-year-old Malcolm was released from prison. He went to Detroit, Michigan, to work at his brother Wilfred's furniture store. He moved in with Wilfred, who had also converted to Islam.

This was the beginning of a new phase of Malcolm's life, and he took a new name. Malcolm dropped his last name, replacing it with the letter X. The NOI preached that black people could partially free themselves from the legacy of slavery in this way. The X served as a reminder that most African Americans didn't know their true family names. During the centuries of slavery in the United States, family names were replaced by slave masters' names when blacks were sold into slavery. In response, many members of the NOI chose X as their last name.

CLIMBING THE RANKS

When Malcolm joined the Nation of Islam, the organization had only about four hundred members. Malcolm and others worked hard to spread the NOI's message. The group grew and grew. Malcolm met with Elijah Muhammad, and the two forged a close friendship. Muhammad could see that Malcolm had the intelligence and dedication to go far.

In the summer of 1953, Malcolm was rewarded for his dedication. He was named assistant minister for Detroit Temple No. 1, where he could continue teaching others about his vision. At this time, his message was often hateful. He spoke of all the terrible wrongs white people had inflicted upon blacks. And he preached openly and with rage about his white ancestry. "What shade of black African polluted by devil white man are you?" he asked. "You see me—well in the streets they used to call me Detroit Red. Yes! Yes, that raping red-headed devil was my *grandfather*! That close, yes! My *mother's* father. She didn't like to speak of it, can you blame her? . . . If I could drain away his blood that pollutes my body,

and pollutes my complexion, I'd do it! Because I hate every drop of the rapist's blood that's in me!"

Malcolm was a fiery speaker. He had a way of moving people, of rallying them to his cause. Malcolm's previous life as a street hustler came in handy. He knew how to talk to a wide range of people.

Malcolm speaks at an NOI conference in Washington, D.C., in 1961. Malcolm was a gifted public speaker, attracting followers to the NOI.

He understood the wants and needs of a thief and a drug addict. He had no fear of going into the poorest, most crime-ridden parts of a city.

Malcolm was promoted to minister and was sent to Boston, where he helped to start a new temple. From there, he moved on to Philadelphia, Pennsylvania, to start yet another. Everywhere Malcolm went, he found success. Young, poor blacks responded to his message. The Nation of Islam was growing into a powerful force, and in 1954, Malcolm was sent to Temple No. 7 in Harlem to recruit members there.

MAKING HEADLINES

Malcolm and New York City's Black Muslims made headlines in April 1957. One day, police broke up a fight on the streets of Harlem. They ordered onlookers to move along. But two Black Muslims—including Johnson Hinton—refused to leave the scene. The officers attacked the men with nightsticks, giving Hinton a savage blow to the head.

Word reached Malcolm, and he rallied his fellow Black Muslims. About fifty of them marched to the police precinct where Hinton was held. They stood in a line in front of the precinct. The police told the men to disperse. Malcolm spoke for the group, refusing to leave. He demanded that Hinton receive the medical care he needed.

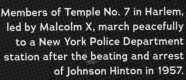

Members of Temple No. 7 in Harlem, led by Malcolm X, march peacefully to a New York Police Department station after the beating and arrest of Johnson Hinton in 1957.

The ranks outside the precinct swelled. More Black Muslims came. So did other African Americans from the neighborhood. "I remember thinking, 'Where did they all *come* from?'" said James Hicks, the editor of the Harlem newspaper *Amsterdam News*. "A movement like that growing up right under your nose."

The police grew nervous. They had heard of the Black Muslims. Rumors said that the group hated all whites and were trained in the martial arts. So the police agreed to send Hinton to the hospital. Malcolm and his Black Muslims moved to the hospital. They refused to leave until they were assured that Hinton was treated. Once they got that assurance, their protest was over.

Hicks described how Malcolm dispersed his people: "Malcolm stood up and waved his hand, and all those people just disappeared. *Disappeared.* One of the police people said to me, 'Did you see what I just saw? . . . This is too much power for one man to have.' He meant one black man. I'll never forget that."

Malcolm and his followers did nothing violent during their vigil. But their display had shown that New York's Black Muslims were a force to be dealt with. For many blacks in the area, this inspired hope. For others, it inspired fear. Many supported the mainstream civil rights movement, which advocated nonviolence. They feared that the more militant movement of the NOI would set back their quest to gain equal rights.

A RIFT OPENS

During this time, Malcolm met a fellow Black Muslim named Betty Dean Sanders. The two felt a connection, began a courtship, and were married in January 1958. In November Betty gave birth to their first child, a daughter named Attallah. Three more daughters—Qubilah, Ilyasah, and Gamilah—would follow over the next several years. (Twins Malikah and Malaak were born after Malcolm's death.)

Meanwhile, Malcolm's work continued. By 1959 he was the leading spokesperson for the Nation of Islam. He was writing a column in the *Amsterdam News*. Later, he helped to start a new newspaper, *Muhammad*

This portrait of Malcolm's wife, Betty, was taken in the early 1960s.

Malcolm holds daughters Qubilah *(left)* and Attallah in 1962.

Speaks, specifically for Black Muslims.

Malcolm traveled around the country—and the world—spreading his message of black power. He told African Americans that they should secure their rights by any means necessary—a stark contrast to the teachings of civil rights leaders such as Martin Luther King Jr., who favored nonviolent methods of protest. Malcolm didn't call for individual acts of violence. He was thinking bigger. He wanted blacks in the United States—and around the world—to rise up together to demand their rights. It was about revolution. And he didn't believe that change could come peacefully.

"Revolution is bloody," Malcolm said in a speech. "Revolution is hostile. Revolution knows no compromise. Revolution overturns and destroys everything that gets in its way." It was a threatening message at a time of highly charged politics and of racial tension. It also made Malcolm a media sensation. Almost overnight, he had become one of the leading figures in the civil rights movement, drawing converts to the NOI. Yet with his success, a rift began to grow between Malcolm and Elijah Muhammad. Malcolm's public statements weren't always in line with Muhammad's vision, which favored a more conservative approach to racial equality. Muhammad and the other leaders of the NOI began to realize they could no longer control Malcolm. He had his own agenda.

By the early 1960s, Malcolm's speeches were drawing thousands. Among the crowds were agents from the Federal Bureau of Investigation (FBI). The U.S. government had been growing uneasy with Malcolm's message of revolution. The FBI reportedly paid informants within the Nation of Islam for updates on Malcolm's plans.

Malcolm's high profile was proving to be problematic for Muhammad. Many in the NOI had become concerned about the amount of power and attention Malcolm had gained. Muhammad's health was in decline, and he wanted his sons to take over as the leaders of the organization. The seeds of distrust between the two men continued to grow.

Wallace Muhammad, Elijah's son, later commented on the disintegration of the friendship between Malcolm and his father. "He [Elijah] actually began to believe that Malcolm was a threat," Wallace said. "And I think that once *he* believed it and Malcolm saw that he was suspicious, then I think that Malcolm began to work secretly to preserve

Malcolm holds up a copy of the NOI newspaper, *Muhammad Speaks*, at a rally in New York City in the early 1960s.

his leadership in the Nation of Islam, and he did become a threat. . . .
Once that support [from Elijah] goes, then Malcolm had a right to feel
fear, because those people [other high-ranking members of the NOI] were
terribly jealous of him. Not physical fear but fear of losing his position.
Because his position was his life. Preaching what he believed in, that was
his life."

1963

In August 1963, Martin Luther King Jr. and other civil rights leaders
planned a peaceful march on Washington, D.C. The march was
designed to show unity among all supporters of civil rights. It would
also send a powerful message to lawmakers to support civil rights
legislation. Malcolm and the Nation of Islam wanted nothing to do with
the march. Malcolm dismissed it as a farce.

The march took place on August 28, 1963, and is best remembered for
King's famous "I have a dream" speech. Yet the event sickened Malcolm.
He was furious with the people who organized it, all the way from King to
President Kennedy. King's nonviolent methods were winning the hearts of
most African Americans. Malcolm did not like that he and the NOI were
being pushed aside in the struggle for equal rights.

Most people in the civil rights movement supported President Kennedy.
When he was assassinated on November 22, 1963, the nation united in
deep mourning. The Nation of Islam issued condolences to the Kennedy
family and ordered NOI ministers not to comment publicly on the
assassination.

But on December 1, Malcolm was asked for his opinion on the killing.
He ignored orders and spoke his mind. In his statements, Malcolm said
that President Kennedy had been commander in chief while the United
States carried out political assassinations during the Vietnam War (1959–
1975). He went on to say that Kennedy "never foresaw that the chickens
would come home to roost so soon." The expression implied that Kennedy
had it coming.

Politically, it was exactly the wrong thing to say. Increasingly on the

A group of mourners gather outside of the hospital in Dallas, Texas, where President Kennedy died on November 22, 1963.

fringes of the civil rights movement, Malcolm had just further alienated himself from mainstream African Americans, who strongly supported Kennedy. Muhammad was furious. He publicly reprimanded Malcolm and officially silenced him for ninety days.

ON A GREATER SCALE

With the punishment, it became clear that Malcolm's days with the NOI were numbered. He began making plans to leave the organization. On March 8, 1964, Malcolm made his plans public. He announced a formal split with the Nation of Islam. He was ready to join the larger civil rights movement, he said—something that he'd been prevented from doing while tied to the Nation of Islam. "It is going to be different now," Malcolm said. "I'm going to join in the fight wherever Negroes ask for my help, and I suspect my activities will be on a greater and more intensive scale than in the past."

Malcolm started a new organization called the Muslim Mosque, Inc. He later started another, the Organization of Afro-American Unity (OAAU). Its goal was to unite blacks in Africa and the United States. He frequently used the term *black nationalism* (later *black power*) to refer to his dream that blacks would one day be part of a global community, separate from whites, with common goals. The term not only summed up Malcolm's goals, it also served as a rallying cry.

As he was branching out, Malcolm wanted to learn more about his Islamic faith. He decided to travel to Mecca, Saudi Arabia, the holy city of Islam. For a Muslim, the pilgrimage to Mecca—called the hajj—is a momentous and sacred event. Malcolm left for Mecca in April 1964. He first traveled to Egypt, where he met with and joined a group of fellow pilgrims. As they traveled, Malcolm noted that pilgrims came in all colors. Malcolm spoke with white Muslims and saw that his hatred of whites had nothing to do with their skin color. It was their prejudicial attitudes toward blacks that he hated. This revelation changed Malcolm's views about himself and his beliefs. The Nation of Islam taught that whites were inherently evil. Suddenly, Malcolm realized that this wasn't true.

A fellow pilgrim later asked Malcolm what had most impressed him about his pilgrimage. He answered, "The *brotherhood*! The people of all races, colors, from all over the world coming together as one! It has proved to me the power of the One God."

Malcolm *(left)* talks to Saudi Arabia's Prince Faisal in 1964 after Malcolm's pilgrimage to Mecca. Malcolm was treated as a special guest by the royal family of Saudi Arabia, adding to the feeling of brotherhood he experienced during his hajj.

A DANGEROUS HOPE

Malcolm returned to the United States having taken a new Islamic name, El-Hajj Malik El-Shabazz. (Betty and their children also took the last name Shabazz.) He came back with a new hope of world

"Whites can help us, but they can't join us. There can be no black-white unity until there is first some black unity. . . . We cannot think of uniting with others until we have first united among ourselves."   **MALCOLM X, JANUARY 1965**

Malcolm X meets Martin Luther King Jr. *(left)* in Washington, D.C., in 1964. Starting in that year, Malcolm's philosophy on using violence to achieve racial equality softened, moving him closer to the mainstream civil rights movement led by King.

brotherhood. No longer did he preach about the separation of the races. Instead, he turned his anger toward the discrimination and prejudice in the United States that fostered division and racial hatred. He vowed to work with whites, so long as they were sincere in their desires to help blacks attain equal rights. He also believed in African unity and traveled to Africa to attend a conference on the matter.

Many people saw Malcolm's message of racial cooperation and African unity as dangerous. For example, the NOI was furious with Malcolm for departing from their message. The mainstream civil rights movement did not embrace him either, seeing him as too radical. In addition, the U.S. government had long distrusted him and continued to monitor his activities. As a result of this alienation, Malcolm's audiences dwindled and death threats came almost daily. None of this stopped him from spreading his message.

CHAPTER 2
A RACIST NATION

It is evident that we [African Americans] can be
improved and elevated only just so fast and far
as we shall improve and elevate ourselves.

FREDERICK DOUGLASS, FORMER SLAVE
AND ABOLITIONIST, 1848

Malcolm X rose to power during a time of great turmoil in the civil rights movement and the struggle for equal treatment of African Americans in the United States. Malcolm's view that the only way African Americans could gain their rights was to take them by force wasn't always popular. Many Americans feared racial war, and others worried that Malcolm's harsh words would slow the pace of progress. Malcolm's bold calls for action, along with his hateful speech about whites, were both shocking and revolutionary. Yet it came out of the nation's long, ugly history of slavery.

THE SLAVE TRADE

One of the main tenets of the Nation of Islam was that white people were devils. Followers of the group pointed to the slave trade as history's greatest crime and as proof of their claim that whites were evil. Slavery is a brutal system of enslaving human beings. It has existed since the dawn of civilization. The ancient Egyptians used slave labor, as did the Greeks, Romans, Chinese, Africans, and many other cultures. The North American slave trade began in the mid-1500s. Black Africans were captured in their native homelands. They were transported to North America in the cargo holds of ships, usually under horrific conditions. Those who survived the journey were sold to white colonists, who put them to work in fields growing tobacco, cotton, and other crops. Others became house slaves—butlers, cooks, and housekeepers. The first recorded sale of captured Africans in the present-day United States was in Jamestown, Virginia, in 1619. The British colonists reasoned that the captured black Africans were of inferior intellect and described them as "ignoble savages."

White slave owners often treated their black slaves with brutality. Slaves who defied their owners could be whipped. Or they could be sold off to another owner and ripped away from their families. One of the first major slave revolts on record took place in 1712. Slaves in New York City banded together and turned on their masters. They killed nine whites before soldiers quashed the rebellion. Many slaves took their own lives

Slaves work in a sweet potato field on a plantation in South Carolina in the 1860s.

RISING IN REBELLION

The most famous slave revolt in the United States took place in Virginia in 1831. A slave named Nat Turner believed that God had spoken to him and told him to rebel against his master. So he began collecting weapons and recruiting fellow slaves to fight by his side. The rebellion started on August 21. The slaves went from one southern plantation to the next, killing white slave owners. They passed by the homes of poor whites, leaving the occupants unharmed. But among slave owners, no one was spared—not even children. The death toll was between fifty-five and sixty.

A white militia ended the rebellion on August 22. Their retribution was brutal. Those involved in the rebellion were hanged. Hundreds of other slaves were killed out of fear and retaliation.

Turner, meanwhile, had fled. He remained in hiding for two months. He was caught on November 5. He was tried, convicted, and eventually hanged on November 11.

rather than be captured. Twenty-one of them were executed—many of them tortured first.

As the North American colonies grew, so too did slavery, especially in the South, where conditions were ideal for large plantations. By 1760 an estimated half million slaves worked on southern plantations.

THE END OF SLAVERY

In the 1800s, the new United States faced a serious division about slavery. Northern states had outlawed slavery and wanted to do the same nationwide. On the other hand, the economy of the southern states depended on slave labor. These states argued against outlawing slavery by stating that individual states should have the power to make their own decisions about slavery.

With the 1860 election of President Abraham Lincoln—an outspoken opponent of slavery—the southern states felt themselves backed into a corner. Seven southern states seceded (withdrew) from the Union, and more soon followed. These thirteen states formed the Confederate States of America, where slavery would remain legal. When Confederate forces fired on U.S. troops at Fort Sumter, South Carolina, the Civil War (1861–1865) began.

The war was about many things but none more central than the issue of slavery. It was not, however, about equality. For example, in the North,

FREDERICK DOUGLASS

Few slaves ever had a chance to voice their opposition to the institution of slavery. But Frederick Douglass (below) did. When Douglass was a child, his wife's master taught him to read. That was very rare, and it set him on a course that would help to change the way many people viewed slavery in the United States.

In 1838 Douglass escaped from slavery in Maryland. He dressed as a sailor and boarded a train north. There, he lectured about the evils of slavery and became a leader in the abolitionist movement to end slavery. To many, he was the voice of the movement. He fought for education for blacks and for women's rights. He was instrumental in making it possible for blacks in the North to fight in the Civil War. He was a prolific antislavery writer. His best-known work is his 1845 autobiography *Narrative of the Life of Frederick Douglass, an American Slave*. Douglass later ran several abolitionist newspapers. His own paper became a major voice in the abolitionist movement.

President Abraham Lincoln *(center)* and two officers pose for a photograph at a Union army camp in Maryland in 1862. The election of Lincoln in 1860 outraged many southerners and led to the Civil War.

blacks turned out by the tens of thousands to sign up to fight with the Union army. But the Union army was segregated (separated by race), so some were turned away, while others were assigned to divisions for blacks only.

Toward the middle of the war, on January 1, 1863, President Abraham Lincoln issued the Emancipation Proclamation, a document that freed all slaves in the Confederacy. The North won the war in 1865. To be allowed back into the Union, southern states had to first give black men the right to vote. Finally, on December 18, 1865, the Thirteenth Amendment to the U.S. Constitution formally outlawed slavery nationwide. But the struggle for equality was far from over.

LIVING FREE

With the Thirteenth Amendment, the nation's roughly four million former slaves were free. Yet many former slaves had nowhere to go. The plantations where they had lived and worked were the only homes they'd ever known. They had no formal education, and few had marketable skills. With the southern economy in ruins, few jobs were available for blacks or whites. So some freed blacks headed north, only to find that there

WHAT'S IN A NAME?

Many members of the NOI, including Malcolm, replaced their family names with the letter *X*. If a member shared the same first name as another member, he or she took on the last name 2X, 3X, and so on. They did this because they felt their original family names were a mark of slavery. And indeed, plantation owners had stripped slaves of their African names. They gave them European names instead. Often slaves took on the last names of their owners. This is likely where Malcolm's family name *Little* came from. When slavery was abolished in the United States in 1865, few slaves knew their original family names. That information had been lost over generations, so they kept the names they had inherited. The NOI's X was a symbol of the many lost names.

was no work there either—and what jobs there were tended to go to whites. Other newly freed slaves stayed in the South and worked as sharecroppers, farming land owned by someone else.

This photo from the 1860s shows a temporary village for homeless former slaves in Virginia after the Civil War. Newly freed blacks found that new laws guaranteeing freedom and equality did not mean freedom from discrimination in everyday life.

In 1868 the U.S. Congress passed the Fourteenth Amendment, which guarantees citizenship and equal protection under the law to all people born in the United States. That same year, Congress passed the Fifteenth Amendment, which guarantees all citizens the right to vote. These laws were largely ignored, however, especially in the South. Many southern states passed laws to block blacks from voting. For example, some states required voters to pay a poll tax, a fee for voting that most blacks couldn't afford. Meanwhile, white supremacist groups such as the Ku Klux Klan organized to violently intimidate any black person who tried to improve his or her social standing.

Southern states also enacted so-called Jim Crow laws to undermine the social and civil gains blacks had made. Technicalities and loopholes all but wiped out the benefits of the Fourteenth and Fifteenth Amendments. For example, in 1867, an estimated 67 percent of eligible southern black voters had registered. By 1882 that number had dropped to 6 percent. Jim Crow laws and fear of retaliation from groups such as the KKK drove away all but the most determined black voters.

Segregation called for "separate but equal" facilities such as drinking fountains and restaurants for blacks and whites. In practice, the facilities were always separate but rarely equal.

Many blacks left the South anticipating better treatment in the North. While the racism in the North may have been less blatant, it was no less real. Northern states and cities had their own versions of Jim Crow laws. The term *separate but equal* became a rallying cry among those eager to keep blacks out of their favorite restaurants, train cars, and other public facilities.

EQUALITY IN THE NEW CENTURY

The fight for racial equality under the law continued into the new century. New voices arose. For example, in 1906 W. E. B. Du Bois, a black sociologist, helped to form the Niagara Movement, which later became the National Association for the Advancement of Colored People (NAACP). The organization fought to end racial discrimination, segregation, and racial violence.

In the mid-1930s, U.S. president Franklin D. Roosevelt set up a group of black advisers, which he called his Black Cabinet, to advise him on civil rights issues. He also instructed the Justice Department to enforce laws that protected the rights of African Americans in the South. These were small but very real steps toward equal rights.

After World War II, in which many black soldiers had fought alongside white soldiers, the U.S. Army finally ended its practice of racial segregation. Attitudes were changing. The stage was set for the civil rights movement to take off.

GAINING STEAM

Many people point to a U.S. Supreme Court case as the moment where the civil rights movement in the United States took off. The case, called *Brown vs. Board of Education of Topeka*, challenged the idea that segregated educational institutions for blacks and whites were legal.

This story began in 1951, when a group of black parents sued the Topeka, Kansas, board of education, demanding that their children be allowed access to the same schools as white students. The case rose all the way to the U.S. Supreme Court. In 1954 the Court ruled unanimously that "separate but equal" segregation was unconstitutional. Blacks had the legal right to attend the same schools as whites.

The decision was a major victory, and it fueled the civil rights movement. In 1955, for example, Rosa Parks, a secretary in Montgomery, Alabama, made headlines when she refused to follow a law that said blacks had to give up their seats to whites on a public bus. Her protest became a symbol of the movement.

Dr. Martin Luther King Jr., a southern minister, helped to organize a bus boycott in Montgomery. The boycott lasted more than a year and ultimately brought an end to racial segregation on the city's buses. King's passion and speaking talent made him a natural leader for the civil rights movement.

This 1953 photograph shows the parents and students involved in the *Brown vs. Board of Education of Topeka* case. The unanimous Supreme Court decision in the case declared "separate but equal" segregation unconstitutional and ended racial segregation in public schools.

Black residents of Montgomery, Alabama, walk to work during the 1955 bus boycott protesting segregation on city buses. It took a year to see the results of this peaceful protest.

King was a deeply religious man. He favored a strictly nonviolent approach to protest. He borrowed this approach from Mohandas Gandhi, the legendary leader of India's movement for independence in the 1930s and the 1940s.

King's messages of nonviolence and civil disobedience (the act of nonviolently defying unjust laws) resonated in the South. However, many activists in northern states—especially young black men—preferred a more direct approach. The messages of Elijah Muhammad and, later, Malcolm X appealed to many of them. They believed that true change was born of action and bloodshed.

In time, King's message won the hearts of the masses. He and the NAACP continued to challenge segregation in and out of the courts. Media coverage of African Americans peacefully protesting—and often facing brutal retaliation from southern whites—went a long way to winning the support of whites in the North. In 1963 King helped to organize the famous march on Washington, D.C., where his "I have a dream" speech moved the world.

STANDING OPPOSED

Malcolm X was one of King's biggest critics. When Malcolm spoke to his followers, he often explained why he thought his way was better. Of King and other civil rights leaders, Malcolm said, "They're just there to restrain you and me, to restrain the struggle. Whereas you and I . . . want to smash everything that gets in our way."

Malcolm's eagerness to speak his mind was both a strength and a weakness. It was his passion and intensity that drew followers to him. But those traits also made him difficult to handle. After Malcolm's controversial comments about the assassination of President Kennedy, the Nation of Islam knew it was time to try to muzzle its most famous member. The rift that had already opened between Muhammad and Malcolm grew wider. In time, it would make Malcolm the enemy of the organization he had done so much to build.

CHAPTER 3
VIOLENT OPPOSITION

Maybe I was manipulated. Maybe I was a pawn—I don't know.
I didn't see it that way at the time. I just believed, man, and
I was the type of person that if I had to stand up for what I
believed, I would do it. I would go all the way.

TALMADGE HAYER, ONE OF MALCOLM X'S ASSASSINS, 1979

Malcolm's assassination, his killers, the details of their plot, and their individual motives still remain wrapped in mystery. Some believe that the official story—that the Nation of Islam had Malcolm killed to silence him—is nothing but a government coverup. But even among those who do believe the official tale, doubt still clouds the story. Who exactly was involved in the killing? How many people were involved? How high up the ranks of the NOI did the plot go, if there was one?

The official story of the prosecution is that three men—Talmadge Hayer, Norman 3X Butler, and Thomas 15X Johnson—conspired to kill Malcolm X. Hayer's involvement is the only certainty. He was caught at the scene and later confessed to being involved. But clarity ends there. Butler and Johnson were both eventually convicted of the crime. But since their 1966 trial, their involvement has come under serious question. Sworn statements by Hayer point to other coconspirators. And even after decades in prison, both Butler and Johnson maintained their innocence—even when doing so was of no obvious gain to either man.

A TWISTED PLOT

Even after his imprisonment, Hayer insisted that Butler and Johnson had not been involved in Malcolm X's assassination. He swore that his coconspirators were actually Leon David, Wilbur McKinley, and William Bradley—members of an NOI mosque in Newark, New Jersey. Investigators followed up on Hayer's claims but found no evidence to pursue charges against the three men. Nonetheless, Hayer has continued to maintain that he, McKinley, and Bradley first started talking about killing Malcolm in the spring of 1964. At that time, Malcolm was traveling around the world, and his public appearances generally had good security. The time would not be right immediately. So the conspirators met often, discussing what they knew about Malcolm and his schedule and whereabouts. They considered killing Malcolm at his home but rejected the idea, fearing that Malcolm's security there would be too tight.

When they learned of Malcolm's upcoming speech at the Audubon Ballroom in Manhattan, they knew their chance had come. Many people believe that to carry out the shooting at the tightly guarded ballroom, the killers must have had help from someone on the inside—someone close to Malcolm. Hayer has never confirmed this suspicion. If, as he says, he and his coconspirators went into the Audubon without any help, it was truly a bold and risky move. "It was just a chance," he told an interviewer. "A long shot, I guess. . . . Why there? I don't know. It was the only place *we* knew he'd be there."

Hayer admits that he bought all three weapons—a sawed-off shotgun, a .45 pistol, and a 9mm Luger—with his own money. Days before the speech at the Audubon, he attended another of Malcolm's events. There, Hayer closely observed the security team and saw that audience members were not being searched for weapons. This convinced him that it wouldn't be difficult to get his guns into the Audubon.

On the evening of February 20, 1965—the night before the assassination—Hayer and his coconspirators went to the Audubon Ballroom, which was hosting a dance. They paid to get into the dance and scouted the location—noting key features such as stairways and exits. The following morning, they met and finalized the plan.

Everything was set. Early on the morning of February 21, the men headed to the Audubon Ballroom.

MUSCLE

In some ways, the early Nation of Islam worked a little like a street gang. The organization had a firm leader (Elijah Muhammad) who asserted his authority and insisted on loyalty and strict adherence to rules. Defection was considered a serious offense. The idea of working with mainstream civil rights groups and using peaceful means was appalling to the NOI. So when Malcolm left the NOI, recruited others to do the same, and then vowed to work with all civil rights groups, the NOI considered this a betrayal of the highest magnitude. The Nation of Islam leadership, from Muhammad on down, seethed with anger.

Malcolm knew that with his shift in philosophy, he would face the

THERE IS NO GOD BUT ALLAH. MUHAMMAD IS HIS APOSTLE

Fruit of Islam members surround Elijah Muhammad for protection as he speaks at a convention in the 1960s.

wrath of the Fruit of Islam (FOI), the Nation of Islam's security force. This group was made up of young NOI members to provide security for members of the NOI. Thomas 15X Johnson later described the FOI:

> We all were in the Fruit of Islam, which was nothing but a paramilitary unit. If someone pulled off a Muslim's bow tie, or ripped up the *Muhammad Speaks* newspaper, we reacted. Tell us to go kick a guy's spleen out, we were on him with all four feet. We were martial artists, but we weren't training to become black belts: We were training to kill black belts. You didn't want to see us coming.

They were coming for Malcolm, however. And he knew it.

TALMADGE HAYER

Talmadge Hayer—the one man everyone agrees was involved in Malcolm X's assassination—was twenty-two at the time of the killing. Born Thomas Hagan, Hayer grew up in Patterson, New Jersey, one of seven children in a poor family. Early in life, he wanted to be someone important—a doctor or a lawyer. But he soon decided that life as a truck driver—his father's job—was a more realistic goal.

Hayer spent a little more than a year in high school before dropping out. He worked in Patterson's textile mills in a series of low-paying jobs, living at home. His parents, who had grown up in the South, told him stories about the KKK and its violent treatment of blacks. This infuriated Hayer. He couldn't imagine why people wouldn't fight back.

By the early 1960s, Hayer had also become a small-time criminal. He was arrested in 1961 for disorderly conduct and again in 1963 for the possession of stolen guns. Meanwhile, Hayer learned about the Nation of Islam. He liked the idea of blacks fighting for their rights. He visited the NOI mosque in nearby Newark and soon converted. "They had their own *army*, man," he told Malcolm X biographer Peter Goldman. "I thought we were going to fight this white, blue-eyed devil."

Hayer was devoted to Elijah Muhammad and felt great anger toward Malcolm over the dispute between the men. According to Hayer, two Black Muslims approached him in 1964. They asked him about his opinions of Malcolm X and wanted to recruit him to be an assassin. This was Hayer's chance to serve the NOI cause, and he wasn't about to pass it up—even though he didn't know exactly where the orders were coming

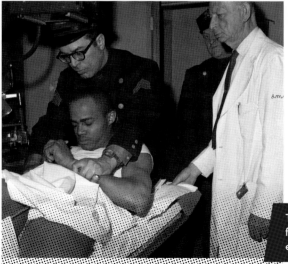

from. "I didn't ask a whole lot of questions as to who's giving us instructions and who's telling us what," he said. "We just knew what had to be done." Hayer (who now goes by Mujahid Abdul Halim) confessed at trial, was found guilty, went to prison, and was released in 2010 after serving a forty-four-year term.

Talmadge Hayer was wounded in the scuffle following Malcolm's assassination. Here, police escort Hayer to the hospital.

NORMAN 3X BUTLER

A tall, muscular karate expert, Norman 3X Butler was a dedicated member of the Nation of Islam and the Fruit of Islam. He lived in the Bronx in New York with his wife and four children and was well known to Malcolm's personal security team. Born in 1938, Butler joined the U.S. Navy after high school. After that, he worked briefly as a security guard, applying to become a police officer. However, because he was open about his membership in the NOI, the police force did not accept him.

In January 1965, Butler and two other FOI members (including Thomas 15X Johnson) were arrested in the shooting of Benjamin Brown. Brown had defected from the NOI. Investigators believed that the attack on Brown was meant as a message to any Black Muslim thinking of leaving the organization. Butler was released on a $10,000 bond (payment to avoid jail time before a trial), with a trial date to be set later.

Police escort Norman 3X Butler *(center)* to jail in New York on February 26, 1965. Butler was one of the suspects in Malcolm's murder.

According to Butler, his legs were injured during his arrest, and severe bruising on both legs backs up this claim. Because the injury hobbled him, it is unclear if he actively participated in the shooting of Malcolm X the next month. Butler maintains his innocence and has said that even if he had wanted to assassinate Malcolm, he wouldn't have been physically able to do so. "I wasn't in [a] condition to do anything," he said. "I couldn't even walk." Nonetheless, Butler (now known as Muhammad Abdul Aziz) was found guilty at trial and went to prison until his release in 1985.

THOMAS 15X JOHNSON

Like Butler, Thomas 15X Johnson was a member of the Fruit of Islam and a suspect in the Benjamin Brown attack. Johnson, too, was well known to Malcolm's security team. This fact has raised questions about how he would have gotten into the Audubon Ballroom without being spotted. Johnson had a history as a heroin addict and a small-time criminal. He had joined the NOI years before, after hearing Malcolm speak at an NOI mosque. Malcolm's words turned his life around, and he became a devout member of the NOI. He found work as a house painter to support his wife and five children, who lived with him in the Bronx.

Johnson was a strong man. He had been a bodyguard for famous boxer Muhammad Ali. Police remarked that at the time of his arrest after Malcolm's murder, Johnson was unfailingly polite, though uncooperative. Like Butler, Johnson maintained his innocence throughout the trial, his lengthy prison sentence (during which he changed his name to Khalil Islam), and in the years between his 1987 release from prison and his death in 2009.

Thomas 15X Johnson *(with mustache)* stands at the police station in New York on March 3, 1965, to be booked on charges of homicide in the murder of Malcolm X.

"I spent most of the day [February 21, 1965] in bed with this rheumatoid-arthritis condition. They said I shot Malcolm, then jumped out the ladies'-room window and ran down the stairs. The truth is, I could hardly walk. . . . I only found out about the shooting when my next-door neighbor came over shouting, 'They got [Malcolm X].'"

KHALIL ISLAM (THOMAS 15X JOHNSON), 2007

CHAPTER 4
GUNNED DOWN

I'll never get old. . . . You'll find that very few people who think like I think live long enough to get old. When I say [to claim our rights] by any means necessary, I mean it with all my heart, my mind, and my soul. A black man should give his life to be free, and he should also be willing to take the life of those who want to take his. When you really think like that, you don't live long.

MALCOLM X, 1964

By early 1965, Malcolm X was a target for assassination. His influence was waning, and he was all but broke. He continued speaking publicly, but his audiences had dwindled. Sometimes the donations he collected weren't even enough to pay the cost of renting the venue.

Friends and family members urged Malcolm to leave New York. But Malcolm wouldn't hear of it. One of his followers later said, "He wanted to die. Malcolm *wanted* to die."

And so, despite every warning sign, Malcolm continued spreading his message to those who would listen. He had a few bodyguards, as well as police protection, but he knew his own death was just a matter of time.

WARNING SHOT

Early in the morning of February 14, 1965, Malcolm and his family were in their Harlem home. Malcolm had just returned from a short trip to Europe. He took a sleeping pill and went to bed. At 2:45 A.M., the sound of shattering glass woke him. Moments later, an explosion rocked the house. Someone had thrown a Molotov cocktail (a homemade explosive) through the window. Boom! Another explosion rocked the house.

Malcolm and Betty—pregnant with twins—sprang out of bed. Already, fire was spreading through the house. As a third Molotov cocktail exploded outside, missing its mark, the family rushed into the backyard. When the fire department responded, the flames were roaring, destroying almost everything the family owned. The children cried as they watched fire ravage their home. Malcolm was furious. He blamed the NOI for the attack. "I have no compassion or mercy for anyone who attacks sleeping babies," he said. In turn, the Black Muslims accused Malcolm of setting the fire himself, all in an effort to gain publicity. They pointed to a bottle of gasoline found in the bedroom of Malcolm's daughters as evidence that Malcolm staged the attack. Malcolm contended that the bottle had been planted there.

DATE WITH DESTINY

Malcolm believed the violence against him would escalate, so he sent his wife and daughters to the safety of a friend's home in Queens, New York. He himself, however, continued traveling and speaking. According to those near him, Malcolm was exhausted and near the point of breaking.

Malcolm arrives at his home on February 15, 1965, the day after it was firebombed.

On the morning of Sunday, February 21, Malcolm was sleeping in a room at the Hotel Theresa in New York. He woke to the ringing of the phone. It was 8:00 A.M. An unknown voice on the other end said, "Wake up, brother." Then the caller hung up.

Malcolm was scheduled to speak at the Audubon Ballroom in Manhattan that afternoon. The Audubon was an important gathering place. Over the years, it had been home to political rallies, music concerts, and parties. Malcolm had spoken before about six hundred people there less than a week before. This time he planned to speak about his goals with the OAAU.

It was a cool February day. Malcolm wore a black cardigan sweater under his suit. He checked out of the hotel at around one in the afternoon

Malcolm speaks to reporters at the Audubon Ballroom the week before his assassination.

and drove to the Audubon Ballroom. He didn't go straight inside, however. People knew his car, and he didn't want to be too easy to identify as he moved toward the building. Instead, Malcolm got into a car with several of his followers—men he identified as his "brothers." From there, he headed into the ballroom.

Twenty police officers were assigned to the event to protect Malcolm. But he refused to allow a police presence inside the ballroom during his speech. One officer stood at the front entrance of the ballroom. Two more were inside in an adjoining room. The remaining officers were stationed at a medical center across the street.

Malcolm's personal security didn't provide much protection either. Nobody searched audience members as they came into the ballroom, and Malcolm had forbade his followers from bringing firearms into the ballroom. (Some of them ignored this order.) Malcolm further ordered that no reporters be allowed inside, though two black reporters were allowed to remove their press badges and come inside.

As the audience filed into the ballroom, Malcolm waited in a back room. He was distressed as he waited. He had asked several other speakers to come, but none of them had shown up. According to Benjamin Goodman, a friend and brother, Malcolm "was more tense than I'd ever seen him. He just lost control of himself completely. I never saw him do that before."

One of the main purposes of this speech was to raise much-needed funds, and Malcolm did not like having to ask for money himself. So instead, he asked Goodman to speak first. It was a role Goodman had played before, and he was ready to do it again.

THE STAGE IS SET

While Malcolm was worrying in the back room, his assassins were taking their places. According to Hayer, he and four other men filtered into the ballroom one or two at a time, hiding their guns under heavy coats. Three of the men, including Hayer, were armed. According to the official report, the other two armed men were Norman 3X Butler and

Thomas 15X Johnson. According to Hayer, they were Leon David and William Bradley.

Charles Kenyatta, one of Malcolm's bodyguards, was concerned about the lax security at the ballroom. He told Malcolm that he felt uncomfortable with the decision to not search audience members for weapons. But Malcolm assured Kenyatta that everything was all right. "I'm with my people here," he said. "I have nothing to worry about."

The crowd settled as Goodman took the stage. Goodman spoke about the cause for about thirty minutes, working the crowd. As Malcolm looked on, he felt uneasy. He told his group that something felt wrong. But whatever he was feeling, he didn't act on it. He signaled to Goodman that he was ready to come onstage, and Goodman quickly wrapped up his speech.

Goodman introduced Malcolm as "a man who would give his life for you," and gave the stage to Malcolm. Goodman later said that he hadn't foreseen what was about to happen—it was just one of those things he said about Malcolm.

Malcolm smiled as the crowd applauded loudly. When the audience began to quiet, he said, "*salaam alaikum*, an Arabic-language greeting meaning "Peace be unto you." The crowd gave the standard response, "*Wa alaikum salaam*," or "And unto you be peace."

BLOOD ON THE STAGE

Suddenly two men in the middle of the audience stood. One of them shouted, "What are you doing in my pockets, man? Get your hand out of my pocket." It was a diversion, designed to draw the attention of Malcolm's security. Several of Malcolm's security guards moved toward the disruption. This was the cue for which Hayer and the others had waited.

On the stage, Malcolm was trying to calm the crowd. "Now brothers," he said, "Be cool, don't get excited. . . ." At that moment, a tall man in the front row stood and drew a sawed-off shotgun. The man quickly leveled the weapon and fired.

THE AUDUBON BALLROOM ASSASSINATION

This diagram shows the sequence of events surrounding the assassination of Malcolm X.

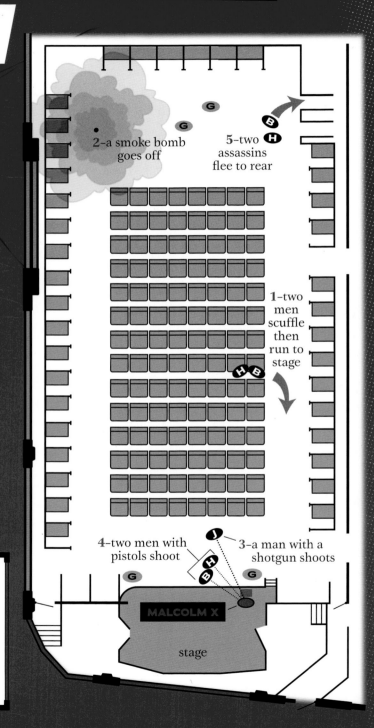

2–a smoke bomb goes off

5–two assassins flee to rear

1–two men scuffle then run to stage

4–two men with pistols shoot

3–a man with a shotgun shoots

MALCOLM X

stage

H Talmadge Hayer
B Norman 3X Butler
J Thomas 15X Johnson
G guard

Feet
0   4   8   12   16   20

0   2   4   6
Meters

THE WEAPONS

Three guns were used to kill Malcolm. The one that caused the gravest wounds was a double-barrel 12-gauge J. C. Higgins shotgun. Shotguns usually have long barrels, but this barrel had been sawed off to make it short enough to conceal inside a coat. The sawed-off barrel reduces the weapon's accuracy at long range. But Malcolm was only 15 feet (5 meters) away from the shooter.

A shotgun shoots a cartridge of many pellets rather than a single bullet. In this case, the shotgun fired twelve double-0 pellets, a type of ammunition called buckshot. Each pellet had a diameter of 0.33 inches (8.4 millimeters)—about the same size as a small bullet. The pellets spread out as they travel, covering a wide range. Buckshot is typically used for hunting large game, such as deer. At close range, victims do not stand a chance.

Talmadge Hayer used a .45 pistol. The *.45* refers to the diameter of the bullet—forty-five hundredths of an inch. The third gun was a 9mm Luger, a weapon named for its designer, Georg J. Luger (1849–1923). Both pistols were automatic or semiautomatic weapons, meaning that an entire cartridge of rounds could be fired with a single pull of the trigger.

Police recovered the shotgun at the scene. One of Malcolm's security team found the .45 pistol, disassembled it, and later turned it in to investigators. The 9mm Luger was never found. Investigators know what kind of gun it was by looking at the bullets that were lodged in Malcolm's body. Any one of the three weapons would have been enough to kill Malcolm. The three of them combined left him no chance of survival.

"There was what sounded like an explosion," said one witness. "I looked at Malcolm, and there was blood running out of his goatee [beard]."

At a range of about 15 feet (5 m), Malcolm never stood a chance. The buckshot pellets blasted through the plywood lectern and into Malcolm's chest. According to witnesses, Malcolm's hands flew up as the impact of the blast knocked him over backward. His eyes rolled back, and blood covered his shirt and his face. It is possible that Malcolm was already dead at this point, but the attack was not yet over.

The shotgun, which had two barrels (firing chambers), fired again. Meanwhile, two other gunmen dressed in overcoats took aim. One gunman was Hayer, who fired a .45 automatic pistol. The other shooter used a 9mm pistol called a Luger. Since Malcolm was already on the ground, most of these shots buried themselves in his legs. The shots created a panic in the ballroom. Audience members—including Betty—dove to the ground. Stray bullets struck two other people. Someone set off a smoke bomb in the back of the room. The assassins used the confusion to dart from the room. The man who had fired first threw the shotgun down and fled. The other two ran through the crowd, waving the guns and ordering people to get out of their way.

"It was a lot of things happening all at once. There [were] chairs falling, people hollering . . . a succession of shots being fired. . . . My babies started crying, and they wanted to know if somebody was going to kill us. . . . Everyone had fallen to the floor, chairs were on the floor, people were crawling around. . . . I looked toward the stage. I didn't see my husband."

BETTY SHABAZZ'S ACCOUNT OF HER HUSBAND'S MURDER, 1965

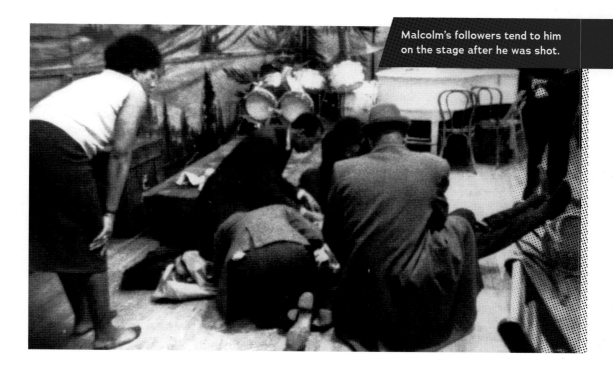

One of Malcolm's followers managed to tackle Hayer, sending him sprawling down a flight of stairs. The .45 pistol fell from his grasp. One of the followers picked it up and tried to fire it, though it didn't discharge. Ruben X, one of Malcolm's bodyguards, then shot Hayer in the leg. An angry crowd had gathered. Had the police not rushed in at that moment, the crowd would likely have killed Hayer. The remaining conspirators slipped away in the confusion.

Meanwhile, others were tending to Malcolm, who lay bloodied on the stage. Staff from a medical center across the street rushed him to an emergency room, where doctors opened his chest cavity and tried to restart his heart. It was a hopeless task. Several of the shotgun pellets had gone through his heart, and after fifteen minutes of frantic work, Malcolm X, aged thirty-nine, was pronounced dead. He left behind Betty, four children, and two babies on the way. According to his lawyer, he left the world penniless, without so much as an insurance policy to provide for his family.

CHAPTER 5
THE AFTERMATH

While we did not always see eye-to-eye on methods to solve the race problem, I always had a deep affection for Malcolm and felt he had a great ability to put his finger on the existence and root of the problem. He was an eloquent spokesman for his point of view and no one can honestly doubt that Malcolm had a great concern for the problems we face as a race.

MARTIN LUTHER KING JR., 1965

After Malcolm's assassination, the New York police immediately launched an investigation. They seemed to have little doubt about who was responsible. The fact that all the suspects were black, combined with the well-known threat from Black Muslims, suggested that operatives from the Nation of Islam had been responsible. The police also suspected that someone from within Malcolm's inner circle had betrayed him. According to investigators, the fact that three armed men were able to so easily get so close to Malcolm suggested that they had an inside contact.

Hayer was captured immediately and eventually taken to a prison hospital ward. Soon the police got a tip about two other potential assassins—Johnson and Butler. Both were suspects in another shooting and had reputations as enforcers for the NOI. Investigators were also interested in Gene Roberts. In photographs, Roberts was standing near Malcolm's body with a gunlike bulge in his pocket. Investigators later learned that Roberts was an undercover police agent who had infiltrated Malcolm's inner circle to keep tabs on him. Roberts was released, and his cover was not blown.

THE RESPONSE

Fearing a riot at the news of the death of a famous black leader, the New York police sent squads into Harlem. Rumors were swirling about retaliation against the NOI, widely believed to be behind Malcolm's death. So the police convinced the NOI mosque there to shut down temporarily. They also sent a warning to police in Chicago, Illinois, where Muhammad lived. The Chicago police responded by sending a security detail to Muhammad's home.

Muhammad and the NOI denied any involvement. "Malcolm died of his own preaching," Muhammad said. "We are innocent of his death." Muhammad said he had no knowledge of Hayer, describing him as a stranger.

Malcolm's supporters were divided among themselves about how to respond. One group mistrusted the police as a tool of white society. They wanted to refuse cooperation. The other group believed that the police investigation was vital to answering the questions about Malcolm's death. Ultimately, distrust won out and Malcolm's supporters were generally uncooperative, which hampered the investigation. "It was hard getting people [witnesses] who had recollections that didn't border on hysteria," said Herbert Stern, the assistant district attorney assigned to the case. "Plus a lot of them were against the system and against whites. They were not accustomed to cooperating with the police."

Also hurting the investigation was the growing rumor that Malcolm's death had been part of a government conspiracy. Even Betty thought that the Central Intelligence Agency (CIA) might have been involved.

"This is the result, it would seem, of a long-standing feud between the followers of Elijah Muhammad and the people who broke away from him, headed by Malcolm X."

SANFORD GARELICK, ASSISTANT CHIEF INSPECTOR, TWO HOURS AFTER MALCOLM'S ASSASSINATION, 1965

CONSPIRACY THEORIES

Almost from the moment Malcolm was killed, questions about who was responsible swirled. The Nation of Islam wasn't the only organization troubled by Malcolm's message. Many believed that the U.S. government had been involved—namely the CIA. The reports of a second arrest at the scene—and the later "disappearance" of that arrest—fueled speculation.

Some people believed that the government was trying to start a war between Malcolm's followers and the Nation of Islam. Both groups expressed hatred of whites and the establishment. Some suggested that there would be no better way to neutralize that movement than to set the two groups to war with each other.

Others think that while law enforcement may not have played an active role in the killing, the police showed little interest in truly protecting Malcolm. With a detail of twenty men, the police not only failed to prevent the murder, but they also managed to capture just one of the conspirators—and only then because Malcolm's security team had first seized him.

Even the police investigators suspected that there was more to the killing than they could prove. Hayer, Butler, and Johnson hadn't hatched the plot. They had merely been the men who carried it out. And they couldn't have done that without help. They shouldn't have been able to get into the Audubon Ballroom armed. Why had Malcolm reportedly ordered that the audience not be searched for weapons on that day? Why had he insisted the police not be inside the ballroom? Why had he been alone on the stage? Some investigators believed that these were not coincidences and that Malcolm had been betrayed by someone close to him. But even that, like so much else about the case, is speculation.

"Normally there were at least four people on the stage with him [Malcolm], but this time, nobody. I think the word was given out to stay away. And how do these three guys [assassins] get in? These men were known to Malcolm's followers, they shouldn't have even been in there, or if they were, they should have been searched. I mean, it all worked too smoothly."

MALCOLM X ASSASSINATION INVESTIGATOR, N.D.

SAYING FAREWELL

By Islamic tradition, Malcolm should have been buried on Monday, February 22, before the sun had set twice on his lifeless body. But this was no ordinary Muslim funeral. It was delayed until Saturday, February 27, so Malcolm's friends and allies from overseas would have the opportunity to come and to pay their respects.

The funeral home where Malcolm's body lay received multiple bomb threats, as did Faith Temple Church in Harlem, which would host the funeral service. Public viewing of Malcolm's body had begun several days before the funeral. About twenty-two thousand people stood in line to pass by the bronze, glass-covered coffin to say their good-byes. Many others sent condolences and words of praise about the man who had opened many minds to new ideas and new approaches to the civil rights movement.

But not everyone was paying tribute to Malcolm. Muhammad and the Nation of Islam were reveling in his death. The day before the funeral, the organization held a convention. They convinced Malcolm's brothers Philbert and Wilfred to speak out against their brother at the event. Muhammad gave a speech thick with self-congratulation and gloating. "We did not want to kill Malcolm and we didn't try to," he told the twenty-five hundred people in attendance. "It was his foolishness, ignorance, and his preachings that brought on his death. . . . I lifted him up and

Malcolm's brother Wilfred Little (who went by Wilfred X) spoke out against his brother the day before Malcolm's funeral.

he came back preaching that we should not take the enemy [whites] as an enemy. . . . It's wrong to stand beside the grave of a hypocrite. He turned his back on the man who taught him all he knew. It was me. Elijah Muhammad. Malcolm got what he was preaching."

The day of the funeral was bitterly cold. People lined up outside Faith Temple Church. Hundreds of police officers were on duty inside and outside the church—including two black officers who stood guard over Malcolm's widow and eight other officers surrounding Malcolm's casket. Bomb threats forced the church to close off its basement, where it had planned to seat the overflow of mourners. Partly for this reason, many who had come to the funeral never made it inside the church.

The service itself was simple. Malcolm's body lay wrapped in white cloth, according to Islamic tradition, while friends and family members spoke. Actor Ossie Davis, a friend of Malcolm's, gave the eulogy. Then

Malcolm's casket was taken to nearby Ferncliff Cemetery, followed by a procession of mourners. There he was to be buried in a grave with a headstone engraved with his Islamic name, El-Hajj Malik El-Shabazz.

As the white gravediggers moved to begin filling in the grave with dirt, Malcolm's followers stood in their way. They announced that white men were not going to bury Malcolm. The gravediggers protested briefly, then handed over their shovels to allow Malcolm's supporters to bury their leader.

PAID ASSASSINS

The police quickly built cases against Butler and Johnson, the two alleged coconspirators with Hayer. Their status as members of the

Ossie Davis delivers the eulogy at Malcolm's funeral at Faith Temple Church on February 27, 1965.

Fruit of Islam, along with their participation in the attack on Benjamin Brown earlier that month, made them prime suspects. In addition, eyewitness descriptions matched, especially for Butler.

On February 26, police detectives went to Butler's home. They found him lying on his couch, seemingly unconcerned about their arrival. The detectives didn't want to arrest Butler on the spot, so they asked him to come with them to answer questions about Malcolm's murder. Butler complied. Once at the station, police put Butler in a lineup and brought in several eyewitnesses to Malcolm's murder. At least two of the witnesses agreed that Butler was the man they'd seen at the Audubon Ballroom. He was arrested, and through several hours of questioning, Butler maintained his innocence.

The case against Johnson was more complicated. Investigators didn't have enough proof against him to move until one of Malcolm's bodyguards, Cary 2X Thomas, decided to cooperate. Thomas, a former NOI member who had followed Malcolm when he'd left the organization, told police that Hayer, Butler, and Johnson were responsible for the murder. That gave police what they needed to arrest Johnson on March 3.

Stern and other investigators were certain that the plot didn't end with Hayer, Butler, and Johnson. Others must have been involved, both directly and indirectly. But there was never enough evidence to move against the people who had planned and ordered the killing. Stern later spoke about his frustrations. "We were dealing with paid assassins," he said. "They weren't giving anybody above them up. You can believe, feel, *know* [that others were involved], but that isn't legal proof."

THE TRIAL

The trial of Malcolm's assassins began on January 12, 1966. The three defendants were tried together, despite Hayer's request to be tried separately. All three men entered pleas of not guilty to the charge of murder. The judge in the case was Charles Marks, who was known to be tough on murder defendants. The jury consisted of nine whites and three blacks, all of varied economic backgrounds.

ON THE BIG SCREEN

In 1992 director Spike Lee released the film *Malcolm X*, based on the autobiography Malcolm wrote with the help of Alex Haley. The film did well at the box office, though it was not a blockbuster. Many critics loved it. Denzel Washington, who played Malcolm, was nominated for an Academy Award. Film critic Roger Ebert of the *Chicago Sun-Times* ranked *Malcolm X* as his number one movie of the year. He wrote, "Watching the film, I understood more clearly how we do have the power to change our own lives, how fate doesn't deal all of the cards. The film is inspirational and educational."

Producer Marvin Worth, who met Malcolm during his Harlem days as Detroit Red, had wanted to make the film for twenty-five years. "It's such a great story, a great American story, and it reflects our society in so many ways," Worth said. "Here's a guy who . . . led so many lives. He pulled himself out of the gutter. He went from country boy to hipster and semi-hoodlum. From there he went to prison, where he became a Muslim. Then he was a spiritual leader who evolved into a humanitarian."

Denzel Washington played Malcolm in the movie *Malcolm X* (1992).

The prosecution laid out its case. They said that Hayer and Butler had staged an altercation in the ballroom so that Johnson could move on Malcolm with the shotgun without being noticed. As soon as Johnson fired, the other two drew their pistols and joined in the shooting. From there, the men fled. The prosecution knew that others might have been involved and that the actual plan was likely much more complicated. But the simplified version would be easy for the jury to understand.

Hayer at first tried to claim innocence but later admitted to being one of the killers. He was not a member of the Nation of Islam, he said, but had been hired by an unnamed organization to perform the hit. Hayer further insisted that Butler and Johnson had not been his coconspirators.

"I know they didn't have anything to do with the crime that was committed at the Audubon Ballroom February 21," Hayer told the court. "I did take part in it and . . . I know for a fact that they [weren't] there. . . . I wanted this to be known to the jury and the court, the judge. I want to tell the truth."

Butler and Johnson, meanwhile, claimed that they'd never even been at the Audubon Ballroom. Their most compelling argument was that as members of the Fruit of Islam, they were well known to Malcolm's security teams. They would never have been able to get into the ballroom in the first place. Butler had the added defense that with his injured leg, he wouldn't have been able to make a run for it after the shooting.

A defendant's likability plays a big role in whether a jury believes that person. While Butler was on the stand, he was hostile and combative toward prosecutors. He made no attempt to be likable. He was flippant in his answers and, at one point, answered a question before the prosecutor asked it. "I know what you're going to say before you say it," he mocked.

Johnson, while more likable on the stand, performed poorly. He claimed at one point to have never handled a shotgun, a rifle, or any firearm in his life. Then later, he said that he had indeed had a loaded rifle in his apartment. When confronted about the contradiction, he replied, "Well, I guess I must have said it if you are reading it from the paper. . . . I must have didn't understand you."

The prosecution had eyewitnesses, including Cary 2X Thomas, who testified that they had seen Butler and Johnson at the scene of the crime. The witnesses helped lay out an easy motive for the murder. Butler and Johnson, they said, wanted Malcolm dead because his message of racial cooperation posed a threat to the NOI. Thomas also challenged Hayer, testifying that Hayer was indeed a part of the Nation of Islam. Thomas's testimony was devastating to the defense, whose case relied on proving that Hayer was not a member of the NOI and that Butler and Johnson had not been at the Audubon Ballroom that day.

On March 11, 1966, after twenty hours of deliberation, the jury returned guilty verdicts for all three defendants. Hayer, Butler, and Johnson were all found guilty of murder in the first degree. A month later, they were each sentenced to life in prison. They would not be eligible for parole (release) for twenty-five years, although that time frame was later shortened.

WHERE ARE THEY NOW?

Despite the accusation that it was complicit in Malcolm's murder, the NOI thrived after Malcolm's death. Elijah Muhammad remained at its head until his death in 1975. His son Wallace Muhammad took over the organization and immediately started to make changes. He rejected the notion that the group's founder was an incarnation of God and worked to move the Nation of Islam closer to the beliefs of Sunni Islam, a mainstream, moderate branch of Islam. He also changed the organization's name to the American Society of Muslims as a way to distance the group from its radical history.

Louis Farrakhan, a former follower of Elijah Muhammad, disagreed with the changes Wallace Muhammad made. Farrakhan led a group that split from the American Society of Muslims in 1977. The new group retained Nation of Islam as its name. In his role as the leader of the NOI, Farrakhan has remained a powerful, often controversial voice in American race relations.

Malcolm's death was devastating for his family. Betty, pregnant with twins, and his daughters witnessed his bloody assassination at the Audubon. They were left penniless, and Betty raised six children on her own. She pursued an education, eventually earning a position as a professor of nursing, and became a college administrator. She died tragically in 1997 from injuries suffered in a fire set by her grandson.

Malcolm's six daughters grew up without their father. Attallah, Malcolm's eldest daughter, thrived. She studied law and became a public speaker before becoming an actress and a director in theater. Qubilah was arrested (and later released) in 1995 on a charge of conspiring to kill Louis

Betty Shabazz attends the premiere of *Malcolm X*, the biographical film of her late husband's life.

"Looking at the Obamas, it's like my father and my mother 43 years later. It was the same old rock star thing, and I think Barack is continuing what my father did with true consciousness, true ability, and a global view. Michelle and Barack epitomize what my father set the stage for—they epitomize global community organizing."

MALAAK SHABAZZ, ON HER OPINION OF PRESIDENT BARACK OBAMA AND HIS WIFE, MICHELLE, 2008

The Shabazz daughters in 1997.
Top, left to right: Attallah, Qubilah, and Ilyasah
Bottom, left to right: Gamilah, Malikah, and Malaak

Farrakhan, whom she blamed for her father's murder. Her son, Malcolm, was convicted of setting the fire that ultimately took Betty Shabazz's life. Ilyasah wrote a book, *Growing Up X*, about living as the daughter of a legendary figure. The book earned her a NAACP Image Award nomination. Gamilah became a rapper. Malikah became an educator and proponent of children's issues. Malaak works with the United Nations, an international peacekeeping organization.

All three men convicted in Malcolm X's assassination were eventually released from prison. Butler was paroled in 1985. He has remained active in the NOI and in 1998 became head of the Nation of Islam's Harlem mosque. He continues to claim his innocence in the killing.

Johnson, who was paroled in 1987, also maintains his innocence. While in prison, Johnson rejected the teachings of the NOI. He converted to Sunni Islam and died in 2009 of natural causes.

Hayer was approved for a work release program in 1988. He spent his weekends in prison, living at home and working during the week. He also pursued an education while in prison, earning a master's degree. He was rejected for parole sixteen times before finally being approved in 2010. He has since expressed regret for his role in the killing. He claims that to this day, he does not know who gave the order for the killing. He sums it up by saying simply, "[I was] part of a machine."

Talmadge Hayer, known as Mujahid Abdul Halim, was photographed while on work release in 2008. He was granted parole two years later.

MALCOLM'S LEGACY

Malcolm X was one of many civil rights leaders—black and white—to pay for the movement with his life. Medgar Evers, a leader in the NAACP, was killed in June 1963. Martin Luther King Jr. was gunned down in April 1968. Senator Robert Kennedy, a presidential candidate and strong supporter and voice for the movement, was shot and killed two months later. These are just a few of the many committed people who died while fighting for racial equality in the United States.

Ultimately, the civil rights movement was a success, due in large part to the sacrifices made by these leaders and their followers. By the late 1960s, African Americans had earned equal rights through the passage of key legislation such as the Civil Rights Act of 1964, which banned racial discrimination in voting, at the workplace, in schools, and in all other public facilities. The Voting Rights Act of 1965 further secured voting rights for African Americans. In 1967 the U.S. Supreme Court declared that state bans on interracial marriage were unconstitutional, while the Fair Housing Act of 1968 banned racial discrimination in housing.

The black power movement, which arose alongside the mainstream civil rights movement, was an extension of what Malcolm X had originally taught. It grew out of the records of his speeches, his autobiography, and interviews he had given. A group called the Black Panthers, formed in 1966, gave the black power movement its most public voice. It was a California-based group of mostly young black men who adopted Malcolm's political stance on race, without the religious component. They supported black pride and social and economic justice, while speaking out against police brutality against blacks. As believers in militant action, the Black Panthers took on Malcolm's mantle after his death, calling for the violent overthrow of racist, segregationist institutions. However, as legal segregation ended and racial tensions eased, the black power movement, too, faded into the background.

In the end, history remembers mainly the passive resistance and nonviolence of Martin Luther King Jr. and his followers. Yet Malcolm rallied tens of thousands of people to action, to fight for their rights and to embrace their African heritage with pride. He urged blacks to insist on an America that saw them as true equals. For this, many remember him as a hero.

THE ULTIMATE JUSTICE OF THE PEOPLE ·

Left: Malcolm's legacy is one of racial pride and equality.
Above: In 1969 Black Panthers protested under a quote
from Abraham Lincoln at a New York City courthouse.
The Panthers were inspired by Malcolm's ideas.

TIMELINE

1925 Malcolm Little is born on May 19 in Omaha, Nebraska.
The Little family, under threat from the Ku Klux Klan, moves to Milwaukee, Wisconsin.

1929 The Little family moves to Michigan.

1930 Wallace Fard Muhammad founds the Nation of Islam (NOI).

1931 Malcolm's father, Earl Little, is killed after being struck by a streetcar. Malcolm's mother suspects that a white supremacist group called the Black Legion is behind the death.

1934 After Wallace Fard Muhammad's disappearance, Elijah Muhammad takes over leadership of the Nation of Islam.

1937 Malcolm's mother, Louise, begins to show signs of mental instability.

1939 Louise is declared legally insane and is committed to an institution. All but her oldest two children are placed in foster homes.

1940 Malcolm moves to Boston to live with his half sister Ella.

1943 Malcolm moves to Harlem in New York and gets caught up in a life of crime.

1945 Fleeing a rival and a dispute over money, Malcolm returns to Boston.

1946 Malcolm is arrested for burglary. He is tried and sentenced to prison.

1948 Malcolm learns about the Nation of Islam while in prison. He writes to Elijah Muhammad and eventually commits himself to the NOI.

1952 Malcolm is paroled from prison. He lives with his brother in Detroit, where he recruits members for the NOI. He changes his last name to X.

1953 Malcolm is named assistant minister of the Nation of Islam's Detroit mosque.

1954 Malcolm spends time as minister of mosques in Boston, Philadelphia, and Harlem.

1957 Malcolm makes headlines by leading Black Muslims in Harlem in protest against the brutal arrest of NOI member Johnson Hinton, insisting that Hinton receive medical care.

1958 Malcolm marries Betty Dean Sanders in January. The first of their six children is born in November.

1963 The NOI officially silences Malcolm after he makes controversial comments about President John F. Kennedy's assassination.

1964 Malcolm announces his formal split with the Nation of Islam. He goes on a pilgrimage to Mecca, Saudi Arabia, and adopts the name El-Hajj Malik El-Shabazz.

1965 Three gunmen assassinate Malcolm at New York's Audubon Ballroom on February 21.

1966 Talmadge Hayer, Norman 3X Butler, and Thomas 15X Johnson are convicted of Malcolm's murder.

1975 Elijah Muhammad dies. His son Wallace takes over leadership of the NOI and later renames it the American Society of Muslims.

1985 Muhammad Abdul Aziz (Norman 3X Butler) is paroled from prison.

1987 Khalil Islam (Thomas 15X Johnson) is paroled from prison.

1995 Malcolm's daughter Qubilah is arrested on charges of plotting to kill NOI leader Louis Farrakhan.

1997 Betty Shabazz dies from wounds suffered in a fire set by her grandson.

2009 Khalil Islam dies of natural causes.

2010 Mujahid Abdul Halim (Talmadge Hayer) is paroled from prison.

2012 The National Trust for Historic Preservation declares Ella Little's home, where Malcolm spent some of his boyhood, to be an endangered historic place. The trust announces plans to renovate the home and turn it into living quarters for graduate students studying civil rights or social justice.

SHORT BIOGRAPHIES

NORMAN 3X BUTLER (B. 1938) Butler, a member of the Fruit of Islam (the NOI's security arm) and a martial arts expert, was a former member of the U.S. Navy. He was under investigation in the beating and shooting of a former Nation of Islam member, Benjamin Brown, when Malcolm was killed. Butler was arrested several days after Malcolm's death. He denied involvement in the case but was convicted and sentenced to prison, where he changed his name to Muhammad Abdul Aziz. He was paroled in 1985. Out of prison, Aziz eventually became the head of the NOI's Harlem mosque in 1998.

LOUIS FARRAKHAN (B. 1933) Born Eugene Walcott in the Bronx, New York, Farrakhan is the leader of the Nation of Islam and a powerful voice for racial equality. Farrakhan was trained as a violinist and by the age of thirteen was playing with Boston-area symphonies. In the 1950s, he was a singer of some note, recording several albums. In 1955 he discovered the Nation of Islam and changed his name to Louis X. The NOI demanded that he leave the music world, which he did. He rose through the ranks and became minister of the organization's Boston mosque and later of the Harlem mosque. His vindictive words about Malcolm X after Malcolm's split with the NOI led many to blame him for the killing. In 1981 he started a new Nation of Islam and continues to be active with the organization. In 1995 Malcolm's daughter Qubilah Shabazz was arrested for taking part in a plot to kill him.

TALMADGE HAYER (B. CA. 1943) The only man to confess to killing Malcolm X, Hayer grew up in Patterson, New Jersey. A high school dropout, Hayer worked at several low-paying jobs before discovering and joining the Nation of Islam in the early 1960s. After the assassination, Hayer was caught by Malcolm X's security team, shot in the leg, and captured by police. He eventually pled guilty and was sentenced to prison. He was paroled in 2010. While in prison, he changed his name to Mujahid Abdul Halim.

THOMAS 15X JOHNSON (1935–2009) Johnson was a small-time criminal and a heroin addict before joining the Nation of Islam. Johnson was found guilty in the assassination of Malcolm X and was sent to prison, despite his insistence that he had not been involved. While in prison, he changed his name to Khalil Islam and rejected the teachings of the NOI, embracing mainstream Sunni Islam. He was paroled in 1987 and died in 2009 of natural causes. To the day of his death, he denied killing Malcolm X.

MARTIN LUTHER KING JR. (1929–1968) King is considered the leader of the civil rights movement. Born in Atlanta, Georgia, he became a Baptist minister. He rose to fame when he led the Montgomery, Alabama, bus boycott of 1955. He led the famous 1963 March on Washington, where he gave his memorable "I have a dream" speech. In 1964 he became the youngest person to win the Nobel Peace Prize. King modeled his nonviolent approach to social change on that of India's Mohandas Gandhi, even traveling to India to meet with Gandhi's family. King was gunned down in Memphis, Tennessee, in 1968. In 1986 Martin Luther King Jr. Day became a national holiday, observed on the third Monday of January.

ELIJAH MUHAMMAD (1897–1975) The controversial leader of the Nation of Islam from 1934 until his death in 1975, Muhammad was born Elijah Poole in Sandersville, Georgia. His parents were sharecroppers (farmers), and his father also served as a Baptist minister. Muhammad married Clara Evans in 1917, and in 1923, they moved to Michigan. The couple had eight children, and Muhammad struggled to find work to support the family. In 1931 he attended a speech by Wallace Fard Muhammad. He soon converted to Islam and became one of Wallace Muhammad's top pupils. He took over leadership of the NOI after Wallace Muhammad's disappearance in 1934. He helped grow the organization and spread its influence across the North. Among the many young black men he mentored were Malcolm X, Louis Farrakhan, and the famous boxer Cassius Clay. He gave Clay his Islamic name, Muhammad Ali. Many believe Muhammad gave the order to have Malcolm X killed, but nothing was ever proven. Muhammad died in 1975 of heart failure.

WALLACE FARD MUHAMMAD (CA. 1893–?) Little is known about the early life of the founder of the Nation of Islam, including his place of birth. By the 1920s, he was living in Los Angeles, California, likely working in the restaurant business. Muhammad turned to crime and served time at San Quentin State Prison from 1926 to 1929. Upon his release, he became active in Islamic culture and started the Nation of Islam. He disappeared suddenly in 1934. No one is sure where he went. The official stance of the NOI was that he boarded the Mother Plane, a UFO.

BETTY SHABAZZ (1934–1997) Malcolm X's wife was born Betty Dean Sanders in either Michigan or Georgia (no official record of her birth exists). She was raised in a foster family from the age of eleven. After high school, she studied nursing. In the mid-1950s, she converted to Islam and met Malcolm X. The couple married in 1958 and had six children, including twins born after Malcolm's death. Betty changed her last name from X to Shabazz after Malcolm's 1964 pilgrimage to Mecca. In 1969 Shabazz continued her education. She became a professor of nursing at Medgar Evers College in New York. Later, she took on an administrative role. In 1997 Shabazz took in her grandson Malcolm Shabazz. A troubled child, Malcolm set fire to her home. Betty suffered burns to 80 percent of her body and later died of her wounds.

QUBILAH SHABAZZ (B. 1960) Malcolm X's second daughter, born in New York, was just four years old when she witnessed her father's murder at the Audubon Ballroom. She went to school in New York and France and in 1984 gave birth to a son, Malcolm Shabazz. By the 1990s, she was living in Minneapolis, Minnesota. Unlike several of her siblings, Qubilah had lived her life mainly out of the public spotlight. But that changed in 1995 when she was arrested for her part in a plot to assassinate Louis Farrakhan, leader of the NOI. Qubilah believed that Farrakhan had been instrumental in the plot that took her father's life. The charges were later dropped on the condition that Qubilah seek psychological treatment. She moved to San Antonio, Texas, where she took a job with a radio station.

GLOSSARY

ABOLITIONIST: in U.S. history, a person who believed in and fought for the outlawing of slavery

AUTOMATIC WEAPON: a gun capable of firing more than one round with a single pull of the trigger

CIVIL DISOBEDIENCE: the act of nonviolently defying laws

CIVIL RIGHTS MOVEMENT: in the United States, the political crusade to secure equal rights, protections, and treatment for people of all races. The movement was at its peak in the 1960s.

CONSPIRACY: a secret agreement between two or more people to perform an unlawful or harmful act

EMANCIPATE: to free someone from something. In U.S. history, emancipation generally refers to freeing someone from slavery.

HAJJ: a sacred pilgrimage to Mecca, Saudi Arabia, the birthplace of the Prophet Muhammad, the founder of Islam. The hajj is one of the most important acts a Muslim can make and is considered a duty of all Muslims who have the means to do so.

JIM CROW LAW: any of a variety of U.S. laws that denied blacks their constitutional rights, often via technicality or loophole

LYNCHING: a mob action of putting someone to death, usually by hanging, without due legal process

MOSQUE: an Islamic house of worship

PAROLE: early release from prison, earned through good behavior or meeting other goals for release

SEGREGATION: a social system that legally enforces separate facilities for different races

SHARECROPPER: a farmer who works a parcel of land and, as payment, shares the crops with the land's owner

SOURCE NOTES

4   Peter Goldman, *The Death and Life of Malcolm X* (Urbana: University of Illinois Press, 1979), 278.

5   Theodore Jones, "Malcolm Knew He Was a 'Marked Man,'" *New York Times*, February 22, 1965, http://www.nytimes.com/learning/general/onthisday/big/0221.html (June 1, 2010).

8   Goldman, *Death and Life*, 6.

17 Malcolm X and Alex Haley. *The Autobiography of Malcolm X* (New York: Ballantine Books, 1999), 135.

18 Ibid., 40.

21 Ibid., 206.

23 Goldman, *Death and Life*, 58.

23 Ibid., 59.

24 Walter Dean Myers, *Malcolm X: By Any Means Necessary* (New York: Scholastic: 1993), 107.

25–26 Goldman, *Death and Life*, 412.

26 Myers, *Any Means Necessary*, 140.

27 George Breitman, *The Last Year of Malcolm X: The Evolution of a Revolutionary* (New York: Pathfinder Press, 1967), 20.

28 Malcolm X and Alex Haley, 345.

29 Breitman, *Last Year*, 45.

30 Jules Archer, *They Had a Dream: The Civil Rights Struggle from Frederick Douglass to Marcus Garvey to Martin Luther King and Malcolm X* (New York: Penguin Books, 1993), 59.

32 Ibid., 2.

41 Ibid., 28.

42 Goldman, *Death and Life*, 416.

44 Ibid., 417.

46 Mark Jacobson, "The Man Who Didn't Shoot Malcolm X," *New York Magazine*, September 30, 2007, http://nymag.com/news/features/38358 (August 2, 2012).

47 Goldman, *Death and Life*, 415.

47 Ibid., 416.

48 Ibid., 420.

49 Jacobson.

50 Goldman, *Death and Life*, 238.

51 Ibid., 5.

52 Ibid., 265.

53 Ibid., 268.

54 Ibid., 270–271.

55 Ibid., 271.

55 Ibid., 273.

55 Ibid.

55 *Time*, "Races: Death and Transfiguration," March 5, 1965, http://www.time.com/time/magazine/article/0,9171,839291,00.html (August 3, 2012).

58 Ibid.

58 Goldman, *Death and Life*, 334.

60 PBS, "Malcolm X: Make It Plain," *PBS.com*, May 19, 2005, http://www.pbs.org/wgbh/amex/malcolmx/peopleevents/e_civilrights.html (August 3, 2013).

62 Goldman, *Death and Life*, 289.

62 Ibid., 295.

62 Peter Kihss, "Malcolm X Shot to Death at Rally Here," *New York Times*, February 22, 1965, http://partners.nytimes.com/library/national/race/022265race-ra.html (August 3, 2012).

64 Goldman, *Death and Life*, 316.

64–65 Ibid., 301–302.

67 Ibid., 315.

68 Ibid., 349.

68 Ibid., 342.

69 Roger Ebert, "Malcolm X," *Chicago Sun-Times*, November 18, 1992, http://rogerebert.suntimes.com/apps/pbcs.dll/article?AID=/19921118/REVIEWS/211180301/1023 (August 3, 2012).

69 Bernard Weinraub, "A Movie Producer Remembers the Human Side of Malcolm X," *New York Times*, November 23, 1992, http://www.nytimes.com/1992/11/23/movies/a-movie-producer-remembers-the-human-side-of-malcolm-x.html (August 3, 2012).

70 Goldman, *Death and Life*, 347–348.

71 Max Blumenthal, "Malcolm X's Daughter Rebukes Al Qaeda Leader," *Daily Beast*, November 21, 2008, http://www.thedailybeast.com/blogs-and-stories/2008-11-21/malcolm-xs-daughter-rebukes-al-qaeda-leader-1 (TK).

73 Goldman, *Death and Life*, 410.

SELECTED BIBLIOGRAPHY

Archer, Jules. *They Had a Dream: The Civil Rights Struggle from Frederick Douglass to Marcus Garvey to Martin Luther King and Malcolm X.* New York: Penguin Books, 1993.

Breitman, George. *The Last Year of Malcolm X: The Evolution of a Revolutionary.* New York: Pathfinder Press, 1967.

Breitman, George, Herman Porter, and Baxter Smith. *The Assassination of Malcolm X.* New York: Pathfinder Press, 1991.

Goldman, Peter. *The Death and Life of Malcolm X,* 2nd ed. Urbana: University of Illinois Press, 1979.

Malcolm X and Alex Haley. *The Autobiography of Malcolm X.* New York: Ballantine Books, 1999.

Myers, Walter Dean. *Malcolm X: By Any Means Necessary.* New York: Scholastic, 1993.

Wilkinson, Brenda. *The Civil Rights Movement: An Illustrated History.* New York: Crescent Books, 1997.

FURTHER INFORMATION

African American World
http://www.pbs.org/wnet/aaworld/
PBS's site, African American World, investigates the history and culture of African Americans, including a wealth of information on the civil rights movement.

Ashby, Ruth. *Rosa Parks: Freedom Rider*. New York: Sterling, 2008. Read about the woman known as the mother of the civil rights movement, her refusal to give up her bus seat, and the impact her brave act had on segregation in the South.

Banting, Erinn. *The Civil Rights Movement*. New York: Weigl Publishers, 2008. Banting covers the civil rights movement, highlighting events such as *Brown v. the Board of Education*, the Montgomery bus boycott, the Freedom Riders, and much more.

Benson, Michael. *Malcolm X*. Minneapolis: Twenty-First Century Books, 2005. This biography of Malcolm X covers every period of his life, examines his message, and looks at the circumstances surrounding his death.

Biography.com—Malcolm X
http://www.biography.com/articles/Malcolm-X-9396195
Check out Malcolm X's biography on the A&E television network's Biography.com site. Malcolm's page includes links to the biographies of related figures, including Elijah Muhammad and Martin Luther King Jr.

Brother Malcolm
http://www.brothermalcolm.net/
This website details the life and legacy of Malcolm X. It includes photographs, speeches, biographical information, a timeline, and much more.

Darby, Jean. *Martin Luther King Jr.* Minneapolis: Twenty-First Century Books, 2005. Learn about U.S. civil rights leader Martin Luther King Jr. in this biography.

Hardy, Sheila Jackson, and Stephen Hardy. *Extraordinary People of the Civil Rights Movement*. New York: Children's Press, 2007. The authors examine the lives and contributions of dozens of civil rights leaders, including Malcolm X, Medgar Evers, and Martin Luther King Jr.

Jeffrey, Laura S. *Betty Shabazz: Sharing the Vision of Malcolm X*. Berkeley Heights, NJ: Enslow Publishers, 2000. Learn more about Betty Shabazz in this biography, which traces her life before, during, and after her marriage to Malcolm.

Landau, Elaine. *Fleeing to Freedom on the Underground Railroad: The Courageous Slaves, Agents, and Conductors*. Minneapolis: Twenty-First Century Books, 2006. This title in the award-winning People's History series examines slave life in the United States and the underground network that helped slaves in the South escape to freedom in the North.

Lindop, Edmund, and Margaret J. Goldstein. *America in the 1960s*. Minneapolis: Twenty-First Century Books, 2010. This book focuses on life in the United States during the 1960s, including coverage of the turbulent years of the civil rights movement.

The Malcolm X Project at Columbia University
http://www.columbia.edu/cu/ccbh/mxp/
This site focuses on new research about the life and mission of Malcolm X. It includes photos, video, quotations, and more.

Nation of Islam
http://www.noi.org/
Visit the Nation of Islam's website to learn more about the history and mission of the Nation of Islam.

Nelson, Vaunda Micheaux. *No Crystal Stair*. Minneapolis: Carolrhoda Lab, 2012. This thought-provoking title explores the life of Lewis Michaux, founder of Harlem's landmark National Memorial African Bookstore. Malcolm X was among the store's many famous clients.

Rubin, Barry M. *The History of Islam*. Broomall, PA : Mason Crest Publishers, 2010. Rubin covers the origins and rise of Islam. He also investigates Islam's place in the modern world and the challenges modern-day Muslims face.

Rummel, Jack. *Malcolm X: Militant Black Leader*. Philadelphia: Chelsea House, 2005. The author focuses on Malcolm's beliefs and his call to arms for black Americans to stand up and demand their rights.

INDEX

ABOUT THE AUTHOR

Matt Doeden is a freelance author and editor, specializing in high-interest children's books. He has written hundreds of books on a wide range of topics, from sports to geography to music to social studies. Two of his sports biographies, *Sandy Koufax* (Twenty-First Century Books, 2007) and *Tom Brady: Unlikely Champion* (Twenty-First Century Books, 2012), have been Junior Library Guild selections. Doeden lives in Minnesota with his wife and two children.

PHOTO ACKNOWLEDGMENTS

The images in this book are used with the permission of: Library of Congress, pp. 1 (LC-DIG-ppmsc-01274), 11 (LC-DIG-fsa-8d28527), 32 (LC-DIG-ppmsca-11398), 36 (LC-USZ62-5334), 74; © iStockphoto.com/sandsun, p. 3 and bullet holes throughout; © New York Daily News Archive/Getty Images, p. 5; AP Photo/Al Burleigh, p. 6; © Michael Ochs Archives/Getty Images, pp. 7, 24 (left); The Illustrated London News, p. 9; © Pat Candido/New York Daily News Archive/Getty Images, p. 12; © Bureau L.A. Collection/CORBIS, p. 15; © Bettmann/CORBIS, pp. 16, 38, 44–45, 46, 48, 49, 52, 65, 66; © Time & Life Pictures/Getty Images, pp. 17, 37; The Granger Collection, New York, pp. 20, 29; Rue des Archives/The Granger Collection, New York, p. 21; Photographs and Prints Division, Schomburg Center for Research in Black Culture, The New York Public Library, Astor, Lenox and Tilden Foundations, p. 22; © Robert L. Haggins/Time & Life Pictures/Getty Images, p. 24 (right); AP Photo, pp. 25, 27; © Pictoral Parade/Archive Photos/Getty Images, p. 28; National Archives, pp. 34, 35; © Carl Iwasaki/Time & Life Pictures/Getty Images, p. 40 (top); © Don Cravens/Time & Life Pictures/Getty Images, p. 40 (bottom); © Judd Mehlman/New York Daily News Archive/Getty Images, p. 47; © Bill Quinn/New York Daily News Archive/Getty Images, p. 53; © Laura Westlund/Independent Picture Service, p. 56; AP Photo/WCBS-TV, p. 59; Courtesy Everett Collection, p. 68; © Robin Platzer/Twin Images/Time & Life Pictures/Getty Images, p. 71; AP Photo/Gino Domenico, p. 72; Splash News/Newscom, p. 73; © Truman Moore/Time & Life Pictures/Getty Images, pp. 76–77; © David Fenton/Archive Photos/Getty Images, p. 77.

Front cover: © Bob Adelman/Magnum Photos.
Back cover: © iStockphoto.com/sandsun.

Main body text set in Gamma ITC Std Book 11/15. Typeface proved by International Typeface Corp.